Noises in the Night

Carmel Reilly
Dee Texidor

Australia • Brazil • Japan • Korea • Mexico • Singapore • Spain • United Kingdom • United States

Noises in the Night

Fast Forward
Yellow Level 6

Text: Carmel Reilly
Illustrations: Dee Texidor
Editor: Kate McGough
Series design: James Lowe
Design: Vonda Pestana
Production controller: Hanako Smith
Audio recordings: Juliet Hill, Picture Start
Spoken by: Matthew King and Abbe Holmes
Reprint: Jennifer Foo

ISBN 978 0 17 012493 5
ISBN 978 0 17 012489 8 (set)

Cengage Learning Australia
Level 7, 80 Dorcas Street
South Melbourne, Victoria Australia 3205
Phone: 1300 790 853

Cengage Learning New Zealand
Unit 4B Rosedale Office Park
331 Rosedale Road, Albany, North Shore NZ 0632
Phone: 0508 635 766

For learning solutions, visit cengage.com.au

Printed in Australia by Ligare Pty Ltd
10 11 12 13 14 15 16 21 20 19 18 17

Evaluated in independent research by staff from the Department of Language, Literacy and Arts Education at the University of Melbourne.

Noises in the Night

Carmel Reilly
Dee Texidor

Contents

Chapter 1

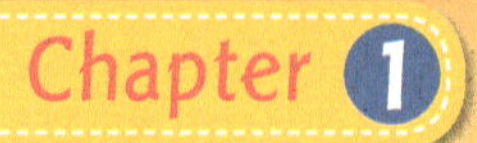

AT CARLA'S HOUSE

After school, Jess went to stay with her friend Carla for the night.

Jess liked Carla's house.

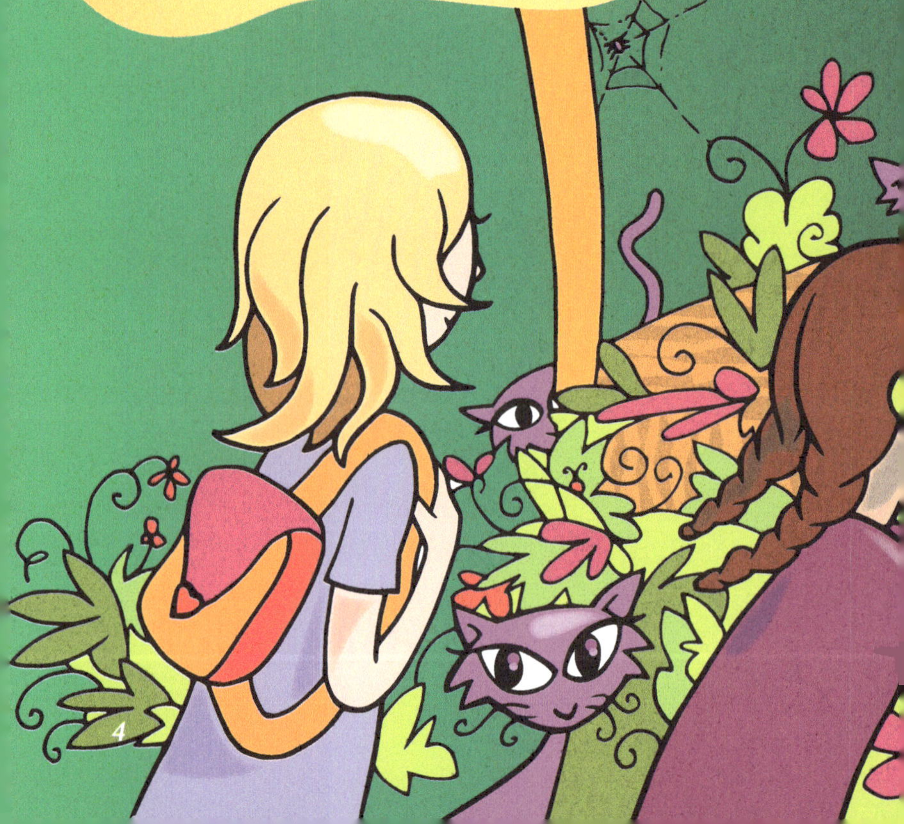

It was big and old,
and it had lots of room
for all of Carla's pets –
three birds, five cats
and one little dog.

After dinner, Carla and Jess
and all the cats
sat and looked at the TV.

Then, Carla's mum said,
"Time for bed, girls!"

The girls went to Carla's room.

"I'm going to sleep," said Carla.
"But you can stay up if you want."

"I will," said Jess.
"I have a good book."

"Good night and sleep well!" said Carla.

"You too," said Jess.

Running Words 104

Chapter 2

A NOISE

Carla got into bed.
But Jess stayed up,
looking at her book.
She did not want to go to sleep.

Jess looked around the room.
Then she looked out the window.
It was a black night.
But ... what was that?

"Carla! Carla!
Did you see that?"
Jess said.

Jess looked over
to Carla,
but Carla was asleep now.

Jess got out of bed,
and looked out the window.

"Oh," she said.
"It is too black to see very well."

Jess was going to go back to bed when she heard a noise.

She jumped.

"What was that?" she said.

"Carla! Carla!" Jess shouted over the room to her friend. "Get up!"

But Carla did not have her hearing-aid in. She did not hear Jess shouting, and she stayed asleep.

Jess stopped.
She heard the noise again.
She stayed very still.

Then she heard the noise again,
but, this time,
it came from outside the window.

Jess looked around.

GET SOME SLEEP!

"Oh!" Jess shouted.
"It's you!"

Sitting at the window
was one of Carla's cats.
It looked like it wanted to come inside.

"Was it you making all that noise?"
said Jess,
as she helped it in.
"What have you been up to?"

Jess got into bed,
and the cat jumped up
on top of her.

"Good night, little one," she said.
"Now all that noise has stopped,
I can get some sleep."